the little book of
self-care

the little book of
self-care

30 practices to soothe the body and mind

SUZY READING

aster

For Dazy

An Hachette UK Company
www.hachette.co.uk

First published in Great Britain in 2019 by Aster,
an imprint of Octopus Publishing Group Ltd
Carmelite House, 50 Victoria Embankment
London EC4Y 0DZ
www.octopusbooks.co.uk

Distributed in the US by Hachette Book Group
1290 Avenue of the Americas
4th and 5th Floors, New York, NY 10104

Distributed in Canada by Canadian Manda Group
664 Annette Street, Toronto, Ontario, Canada M6S 2C8

ISBN (UK) 978-1-78325-305-0
ISBN (US) 978-1-78325-312-8

A CIP catalogue record for this book is available from the British Library.

Printed and bound in China

10 9 8 7 6 5 4 3 2

Consultant publisher Kate Adams
Senior editor Pauline Bache
Copy editor Jane Birch
Art director Yasia Williams-Leedham
Designer Megan van Staden
Picture library manager Jennifer Veall
Production manager Caroline Alberti

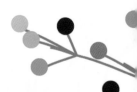

CONTENTS

IS IT REALLY OK TO LOOK

AFTER MYSELF?

We've all heard of self-care and our heads nod
in agreement when we talk of its importance
but, in truth, self-care isn't always easy. As a
concept it's still a bit misunderstood, and in
practice many people feel it's inaccessible or
that they're failing at it. What we all need to
make self-care happen is a practical definition
and a broad toolkit from which to draw. Stick
with me, I know how full life is. My aim in this
book is to empower you by clarifying what self-
care really is and offering a selection of tried and
tested soothing practices that are both potent
and doable.

In the years since self-care exploded onto centre
stage, there have been all sorts of reactions.
Check out the media and you'll find some
interesting commentary – it's just a fad,
it's narcissism or it's well-being gone mad.
On a personal level, there is a chorus of voices
saying "I don't have time", "I don't have the
energy" or "I don't have the spare cash". And the
most tenacious theme ringing through is guilt.

I hear you. Rest assured we will address all these misconceptions and genuine barriers. In fact, when we look closely at what self-care is, when we broaden the concept of what constitutes a nourishing practice and see the true benefits, all these barriers drop away in an instant. You will see how self-care can be the best preventative medicine.

As a practice, self-care can feel confusing and there are good reasons for this. There isn't a "one size fits all" approach. What one person finds soothing might not be a tonic for someone else, and even our own needs and resources naturally change over time. What I see in my consulting room as a psychologist, and from my own life experience, is that the time when we need self-care the most is when it drops away. We don't have the same time, energy and resources available to us during periods of stress, loss and change and in that state of overwhelm we don't have the resourcefulness or creativity to come up with something else. We need a different toolkit when life squeezes us and we need it spelled out because it's hard to put your finger on something nourishing when you're fried. If you're feeling this way you just need a selection of soothing practices and that's exactly what you'll find in this book.

WHAT IS SELF-CARE?

Simply put, self-care is nourishment for the head, the heart and the body. My definition has two parts. Firstly, I always say that self-care is health care – because without our health, what do we have? By health, we are referring to physical health, emotional health, energetic health and mental health. If it's ok to brush your teeth and hit the gym, it is equally ok to give yourself permission to stop, rest and top up your energy bank. I urge you to take a look at your self-care practices and make sure there is something in there for every aspect of your well-being: mind and body. You'll find a wide selection of different practices in this book – some meditative in nature, some using movement, others that harness the mind in a variety of constructive ways. Flip through when you need a moment of nurturing and you will find something that resonates. Every day will be different.

Please don't equate self-care with pampering: it can be pampering but it is not limited to luxurious practices. Sometimes a restorative act is just what you need; in other moments, the true act of self-care might be the last thing you actually feel like doing, something that challenges you or requires you to step up, like sitting to meditate when your mind is whirring or heading out for that jog when the sofa is calling to you.

To make it easier to get clear on self-care there is a second part to my definition. Self-care is health care, *nourishing you in this moment AND nourishing the person you are becoming*. If you're not sure, ask your "Future Self". There is great wisdom to be mined there. The manner of asking will vary from person to person and for you from moment to moment but this definition and a broad toolkit will serve you well.

For those wondering where self-care has come from, let's be honest, there is nothing new about many self-care practices like healthy eating, getting decent sleep or breathing...and as a term it has been around for decades. It was originally used in the context of workers in high-risk or stressful professions needing to look after themselves so they could sustain their care-giving roles. More recently, interest has been driven by research in Positive Psychology – the study of what makes life worth living and of the building blocks of well-being. It is also rising to the fore because as a society we are talking more openly about mental health. Self-care is so much more than a fad.

WHAT ARE THE BENEFITS OF SELF-CARE?

▸ Self-care helps us cope in the moment, whether we're feeling overwhelmed, tired, "hangry", we have to rise to meet a work challenge or we are digging deep to meet our children's needs. Self-care helps us navigate these experiences with a sense of calmness, poise and purpose.

▸ After periods of stress, loss, conflict or change, self-care can put us back together. We all need a toolkit to help us restore, replenish and heal because no one is immune from these experiences.

▸ Engaging in proactive self-care helps to boost our resilience, providing us with a protective buffer against future challenges. Just like a car needs fuel to move, we need energy to get through our day and the greater the reserves in our energy bank the more effective we are. An act of self-care is like a deposit in our energy bank and we need a healthy balance because it's not just crisis and illness that deplete us; things we desperately want – like promotions, having kids, getting married, buying or renovating a house or just planning a holiday – have an energetic tax on us too! Self-care allows us to keep giving and keep going. Energetic bankruptcy serves no one.

▶ And last but not least, self-care gives us access to our best selves. Think of any goal or quality you aspire to possess – you are more likely to achieve it when you are well nourished. Self-care helps us all become kinder, more compassionate people and this benefits everyone our lives touch. This is the win-win that can put guilt back in its place.

HOW DO WE DO SELF-CARE?

THE VITALITY WHEEL

▸ A framework or set of categories can help bring self-care to life, making it easy to pin down an accessible soothing practice when we need it the most. I created the Vitality Wheel – which is informed by Positive Psychology, Cognitive Behaviour Therapy (CBT), mindfulness, Acceptance and Commitment Therapy, yoga philosophy and my decade working as a personal trainer and health coach – for this purpose. The Vitality Wheel shows you eight different ways in which you can nourish yourself and top up your energy bank balance. Looking at the Vitality Wheel will open your eyes to different options, helping you choose something of resonance and circumvent confusion and indecision. It is far more effective than trying to scroll through your mind when you are feeling under pressure.

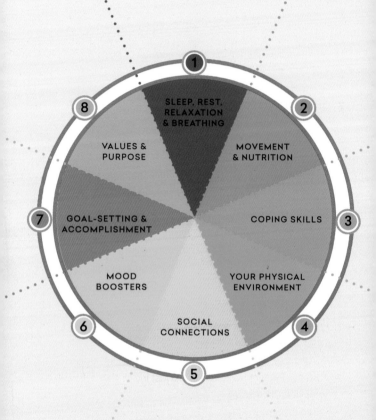

1. Soothe your nervous system by prioritizing sleep, R & R and working with your breath.

2. Eat and move for physical AND mental health.

3. Specific tools and skills to keep your thinking constructive.

4. Harnessing the power of your environment – home, work and the skin you live in, and tapping into the therapeutic effect of nature.

5. Boosting the health of your relationships and deepening your feeling of connection.

6. Skills and activities that lift the spirit.

7. Creating goals that boost well-being and reflecting on what you've achieved to lift your mood.

8. Connecting with what matters most in life and deepening your self-knowledge.

MAKING SELF-CARE HAPPEN

"MICRO MOMENTS OF NOURISHMENT"

▸ Self-care needn't involve large investments of
time. Take the "micro moments of nourishment"
approach and dot them through your day: sixty
seconds of being with the breath; savouring the
scent of your morning coffee; repeating a mantra
to cultivate how you want to feel; a few minutes
to unwind at your desk; ten minutes of soothing
yoga or journalling before you go to bed. The
practices in this book are potent stress busters
and will change the quality of your day, just like
hitting the reboot button.

TURN EVERYDAY ACTIONS INTO SELF-CARE

▸ Become skilled in the art of mindfulness,
curiosity, kindness, compassion and savouring
and this will transform the lens through which
you see the world. In this way we imbue everyday
actions with a feeling of tenderness and care.
What are you already doing that you can make
more nourishing? The way you greet the day,
the way in which you dress yourself, how you

shower, how you eat your meals, the way you talk to yourself. These are all things we can turn into a ritual of nourishment with awareness and choice.

MINDFUL DOWNTIME

▸ Too often we fritter away precious spare moments by scrolling on our phones, overthinking or mindless busyness. Make the most of your downtime and use the Vitality Wheel to choose something truly nourishing. Connect with how you're feeling right now, how you'd like your "Future Self" to be and take loving action.

MAKE AN APPOINTMENT WITH YOURSELF

▸ We book our car in for a service without guilt: similarly, schedule time in for you. If self-care is constantly getting bumped, carve out time in the diary and make it a non-negotiable. There is rarely a "good" time, we need to make time. Whether it is an art class, a session with your osteopath or planning a date night to feed your relationship, give your nourishment the priority it deserves and book it in. Proactive self-care is better than simmering resentment, potential burnout and enforced rest through sickness.

MAKING SELF-CARE A HABIT

▸ If you find it hard to remember self-care, piggyback existing habits with an act of self-care. Every time you drink a glass of water, take the opportunity to stand tall, relax your shoulders and enjoy five deep breaths. Pair another self-care activity to toilet breaks, like using a hand wash with a scent you love. While you're waiting for the kettle to boil take a yoga pose. This is how we build the self-care habit. Keep it evolving to maximize effectiveness.

HOW TO USE THIS BOOK

▸ You'll find a great variety of practices in this book, some that will come naturally and some that might not resonate at first glance. Try them all and see what works for you at different times. Some of the skills-based practices may take a little work and that's ok! Dip in at any page and give it a go. Self-care is most effective when we vary our approach so keep diving back into the book and trying different things. I hope you enjoy exploring these soothing practices and seeing the benefits ripple out to improve all areas of your life.

1. CREATE A SELF-CARE JOURNAL

▸ A great way to start your self-care journey is with a journal to record your ideas, inspiration and experiences. The act of journalling is a self-care activity in itself and reading back through previous entries is such a simple mood booster. To begin the practice, seek out a journal you love the look and feel of, something you feel drawn to picking up and leafing through. This is the place to keep all your goals and insights relating to your well-being. Keep a copy of the Vitality Wheel in it for easy reference. Set the intention to keep this journal as a place for positivity. Writing about challenging experiences can be a very effective way to vent and process our feelings but to maximize the cathartic benefits it is best to jot them down on a spare piece of paper and then relish ripping it up and tossing it away. Positive journalling is writing about uplifting experiences such as moments of awe, hope, joy, growth and gratitude. I like to think of my journal as a "happy memory bank".

To help you wholeheartedly commit to the practice of self-care, brainstorm in your journal the "why" of self-care by reflecting on the following points:

▶ Describe yourself when you are well nourished and topped up with energy. What does this facilitate in your life? What does this allow you to do or be?

▶ Describe yourself when you are depleted, empty or fatigued. How does this affect your life and the people around you?

▶ Write out a few statements of why you personally want to commit to taking better care of yourself – for you and anyone your life touches.

Turn to your Self-Care Journal on a regular basis and ask yourself: *what do I need today*? Use the Vitality Wheel, this book and previous entries in your Self-Care Journal to inspire you with life-giving action.

2. GREET YOUR FEET

▶ Touch can be deeply healing and the self-massage in this soothing practice helps to relieve tension, reconnects you with your feet and helps you feel grounded in the earth.

Find a comfortable seat, barefoot, preferably outside in nature's beauty. Take a moment to look at your feet. When was the last time you really studied them with curiosity or extended a feeling of tenderness toward them? So often they are covered up, relegated to just things at the ends of our legs or, worse, disliked! Marvel at their incredible structure – 26 bones in each foot – and feel a sense of appreciation for what they allow you to do.

Observe the appearance of your feet, in particular the colour of the skin. Notice how they feel from within and, before you touch them, give your toes a little wriggle, feeling their dexterity. Do they all move? Can you move your little toes independently of the others? If you wish, stand up and notice how it feels to be standing, the sensation of the earth beneath your feet.

Once seated again, begin by cradling one foot toward you and rubbing the whole surface area of the sole of your foot with your thumbs, starting at the inner heel, along the instep and out through the neck of the big toe. Continue from the middle of your heel, through the middle of the sole of your foot and out through each toe. Finish with the outer heel, outer edge of your foot and through the little toe.

Next, squeeze your entire foot, top and bottom, firmly with both hands. Start with the toes and work toward your heel and ankle. Finish the massage practice with a pitter patter of your hands across the sole of your foot and then the top.

Now stretch both legs out in front of you and observe the difference between your feet – the colour, temperature, circulation, dexterity, and feeling of control and connection. Feel how this practice helps you reclaim your feet. Balance things out by repeating the sequence on the other foot and, once complete, come back to standing, to feel a greater connection with your body, secure in your grounding.

3. MANTRA: *"I AM. I CAN."*

▶ If you're feeling flustered, repeat this mantra to find peace and clarity. It will help you break things down into manageable steps and galvanize you to beat overwhelm.

The first part, *"I am"*, allows you to own how you feel right now, and to channel how you'd like to feel. The *"I can"* part encourages you to focus on what lies within your control. I like to draw on the *"I can"* to remind me of a strength that will help me step up to meet the demands of the situation.

So, for example: *I am* tired; this might be the honest truth, but I am also resilient and I am motivated. Or I am feeling confused, but *I can* call on my curiosity and resourcefulness to find a solution. Play with your *"I am. I can"* and see what you tap into.

4. TAKE A GRATITUDE WALK

▸ Harness the therapeutic power of movement, nature and gratitude with this mindfulness ritual. Head outside with the express intention of counting your blessings. If there's the opportunity, carve out time to go somewhere special to you and immerse yourself in the beauty of this place. Notice all the qualities that resonate for you and give thanks for them. As you walk, feel the gift of your physical capacity and enjoy the sensation of moving your body. Every time your mind wanders towards worry, negativity or your "to do" list, anchor it back on an aspect of your life for which you feel grateful – the roof above your head, a stable or rewarding career, a rich family life, your health, adventures you've had or travel to come. When life is squeezing you it might feel hard at first to find those blessings, but dig a little and you will always unearth some – maybe it's gratitude for this day or just this breath.

Nothing fancy is required here; if there's not time for a long walk, turn a portion of your commute or a quick walk around the block into a gratitude practice. Take a buddy with you and enjoy connecting over life's joys, celebrating what's going well.

Run a bubble
bath and add
an oil to suit
your mood.

5. MEDITATION USING YOUR HANDS

▶ Many people find meditating challenging – even seasoned meditators! The good news is that there is no success or failure when it comes to meditating – there is just the act of meditating. Even if you don't have a "peaceful sit", the job is done and you have still managed to rewire your brain.

If you think that meditation is not for you, rest assured there will be some meditative tool that will work, it might just take some experimenting. The mind is designed to think just as the eyes are designed to see, so let go of the belief that meditation equates to clearing the mind. Thoughts, sensations, memories, images and emotions will all float to the surface. The key is to acknowledge them without getting wrapped up in them or identifying with them, and then return your attention to the anchor you've chosen. In this meditation practice we are anchoring the mind on a hand mudra (gesture) and feeling the effect this has on your breathing – this one might really surprise you!

Allow yourself time and space to settle, leave your phone in another room and let others know you'll be taking a few minutes for yourself to recharge. Find a seated position that allows you to elongate your spine and sit comfortably for a few minutes. This could be cross-legged on the floor with a bolster beneath your sit bones or in a chair – be guided by your comfort.

Feel the support of the floor or chair beneath you and encourage the crown of your head to snake its way skyward, feeling the buoyancy of your skull. Soften all the muscles of your face, close your eyes, release your jaw and loosen the tongue in your mouth. Let your shoulders drop heavily away from your ears. Spend a minute noticing how it feels to sit still, allowing the thoughts and feelings to pop up as they will.

Now direct your attention to your breathing. There is no right way to breathe and this is not thinking about the breath, this is feeling the sensations of it. Let your breath be exactly as you find it, noticing where you feel it move through your body. It could be your tummy, your sides, your back, your chest and even up into your collar bones. Let it move through you, filling all the internal nooks and crannies on the inhalation and just a gentle, effortless retraction back to your centre on the exhalation.

Now draw attention to the position you've chosen for your hands. Just notice how pleasant it feels for the hands to have nothing to do. Next, place your palms flat down onto your thighs in a way that keeps your shoulders relaxed and allows you to soften the whole length of your arm. Get curious about the effect this hand mudra has on your breathing. What you might notice is that it makes your exhalation longer, deeper or easier. Enjoy ten soothing breaths with the palms facing downward, creating a feeling of grounding and stability. Next, turn your palms to face upward and allow the fingertips to curl loosely toward your palms. Notice how this hand gesture changes the sensation of your breathing. You might begin to feel the inhalation seems lighter, longer or easier. Savour ten smooth breaths with your palms facing upward, experiencing a sense of openness, being invigorated with fresh energy.

Lastly, bring the thumb and first finger of each hand to touch in Chin Mudra. Observe how this hand position changes your breathing. You may feel this directs your breath into your abdomen, encouraging diaphragmatic breathing which is naturally calming and centring. Be here for another ten breaths or longer if it feels good, or return to the hand position that resonates most, anchoring your mind on the sensation of your breath. Every time your mind wanders elsewhere, without criticism, bring it back to your breath.

6. SAVOURING SCENT

▸ Throughout your day, direct your attention to noticing scent and its different energetic effects. There is great pleasure to be mined in everyday experiences – the scent of your shower gel, a spritz of your favourite fragrance, the aroma of your morning coffee, freshly mown grass or your little one's skin. Scent has the power to transform your mood in an instant, whether it be via the opportunity to pause and take a moment to enjoy a deeply pleasurable aroma, by encouraging us to stand tall and take a few restorative breaths, or the scent itself harnessing different energetic effects. Choose peppermint or pine to focus, citrus, basil, white neroli and mimosa to energize and uplift, or lavender or myrrh to soothe and calm. Memory plays a significant part too where particular scents can connect us with treasured times, special people or transport us to precious places. Think about how you want to feel and choose a scent that helps you cultivate that. Remember this practice when you fall into the habit of thinking you don't have time for self-care and turn to scent to channel how you'd like to feel. We all have time for this!

7. FEELING FRAZZLED OR

OVERWHELMED? HIT THE

REBOOT BUTTON

▶ Make soft fists with your hands and press the
bases of your thumbs into your forehead, like
you're making two horns. Feel how this instantly
relaxes your eyes and your jaw and slows your
rate of breathing, soothing your nervous system.
Alternatively, if you are seated at a table, fold
your hands on the table and rest your forehead
on your folded hands. Notice that this posture, or
one in which the back of the hand comes to press
against the forehead, is one you would naturally
come into if you got bad news – the body is
hardwired to help you cope and heal. Turn to
this practice whenever you feel overwhelmed.

8. MAKE A VISION BOARD

▸ Draw on the power of imagery and create a vision board about an area of your life – your home and garden, holidays, health, leisure and fun, career, relationships or family. Sift through magazines, brochures, photos and printouts from the internet and gather together some things that inspire you. Express yourself with a collage of colours, images and words which speak to you. This could be something that you hang on the refrigerator to keep your focus fresh or you can use your clippings to decorate the pages of your Self-Care Journal (see page 20).

Once your vision board is complete, pause to reflect:

- What does your vision board say to you?
- Does it give you greater clarity on what's most important to you?
- What action steps will bring your vision closer to becoming reality?

Keep checking in with your vision board, taking action and imagining how it would feel for these dreams to become reality. Share it with a friend and draw on their support to keep you moving in the right direction. Maybe there could be some shared dreams you can co-create.

9. DESTRESS AT YOUR DESK

- Release your wrists by rotating them flamenco-style five times in one direction and five in the other.

- Take your right arm out in front of your body with your palm facing upward. Using your left hand, gently draw your fingers down and toward you, stretching your palm, inner wrist, forearm and bicep. Hold for five breaths and repeat on your other arm.

- Bring the backs of your hands and fingers to touch in front of your chest in a reverse praying position. Lower your hands toward your navel without letting the backs of your hands separate and draw your shoulders down away from your ears. Feel the stretch in the backs of your wrists and forearms. Take five breaths here, then shake out your hands and re-enter your day with greater vigour.

Buy two
bunches of
flowers – one
for you, one for
someone else.

10. PLUG IN

▸ Social connection literally feeds the soul, and
I'm not talking about social media connection.
Today, set the intention to be in tune with other
people. Just bringing this quality of awareness to
your interactions will provide you with a richer,
more rewarding experience of connection. Make
an effort to be present, to give eye contact, use a
person's name if you know it, to communicate
sincere warmth and interest. Be on the lookout
for opportunities to radiate kindness and care,
without the desire for anything in return. It can
be with those you love or those you don't know
– a passer-by in the street, the postman or the
person serving your lunch. Feel how this fills
your cup.

11. BUILD YOUR OWN CALMING TOOLKIT

▸ Think of any challenge you are facing right now and come up with a path of action. Humans thrive on certainty, so even if you can't guarantee a particular outcome, having a defined toolkit of things to try can be a powerful coping strategy. Think along the lines of: "When X happens, then I will Y..." These primer statements become even more potent when written down and your Self-Care Journal (see page 20) is the perfect place to record these ideas. Creating this toolkit can diminish anxiety and will help you take swift, constructive action when challenges arise.

Let's use sleep as an example.

When I can't sleep, then I will ...

▸ Resist the temptation to look at my phone (it's too stimulating and the light emitted interferes with the production of sleep hormones!).

▸ Put my hands on my belly and breathe into my fingertips.

- Scan my body and release any physical tension I find along the way.

- Repeat a mantra, something like: *"Sleep will come, rest is just as good until then"* or *"There is nothing required of me right now"*.

- Distract my mind from worry about wakefulness by replaying my day in reverse or getting creative and designing my "best day" imaginable.

- If I'm feeling agitated, I'll get up and do something really boring or super soothing, anything sufficiently engaging to distract myself from anxiety over sleep.

- If I can't sleep I will just rest, it's ok.

12. WEAR SOMETHING YOU LOVE

▸ As you dress yourself today, choose something
that makes you feel happy or gives you a sense of
belonging. It could be a colour or fabric that you
enjoy, a particular garment which makes you feel
good or a treasured piece of jewellery. If you don't
have underwear that you relish, please make the
investment for your happiness and well-being!
Mindfully check in with what you are wearing
through your day, like an affirmation of self-
worth, and feel it lift your spirits. Self-care at
its simplest.

13. WANT TO CHANGE YOUR MIND?

MOVE YOUR BODY

▶ How we hold our bodies has a potent effect on
our energy levels and outlook. Lengthening your
spine and broadening your chest is a simple
way to boost your mood and sense of personal
power. If your thinking is sticky, you're fatigued
or having trouble focusing, use the body to shift
how you feel.

Try these easy stretches to improve your posture
and your state of mind:

CHEST STRETCH

Stand with your right-hand side by a wall, raise
your right arm to the same height as your head
and place your right palm flat on the wall. Slowly
turn your feet and body away from the wall until
you feel a comfortable stretch through your right
arm and into the right-hand side of your chest.
Take five slow, deep breaths into the stretch
before changing sides.

UPPER BACK AND NECK STRETCH

Give yourself a hug with your right arm on top of your left. Let your chin drop down toward your chest, and round your upper back. Send a lovely deep in breath into your fingertips and enjoy the sensation of the stretch between your shoulder blades. Take five breaths here before repeating the hug with the left arm wrapped on top.

"CHICKEN WING" SHOULDER ROLLS

Place your fingertips on your shoulders forming a "chicken wing" – silly, I know, but more memorable and more effective than just having your arms relaxed by your sides. Draw big circles with your elbows up, out and down, lubricating the shoulder joints and opening up your body to receive a more expansive breath.

14. SUPERCHARGE YOUR WATER

▶ Turn your hydration into a ritual of nourishment.
To your regular drinking water add a flower
essence, essential oil or crystal with a property
you wish to possess, and focus on it with every
sip. This will not only boost your fluid intake
but can also help cultivate how you want to feel.
Add 2–4 drops of a flower remedy, I like Bach's
Star of Bethlehem to promote emotional healing,
Wild Oat for clarity or Larch for confidence. For
crystal-infused water, add a quality, clean and
charged gemstone to your water bottle or pitcher.
Not all crystals are suitable so check first. You
could try rose quartz for self-love, clear quartz
to boost immunity, garnet for abundance or
shungite to detoxify and cleanse. For essential
oils, use a glass container and mix 1–2 drops of
oil with a dispersant, like a pinch of sea salt,
raw honey, aloe vera juice or mashed fruit, then
stir into your water. Add lemon oil to cleanse
and reduce cravings, grapefruit to refresh and
energize, or lime to lift your mood.

Feeling stressed out? Make your exhalation longer than your inhalation.

15. STAY ANCHORED WITH A TALISMAN

▶ Source an object that has special meaning for
you – maybe because it was given to you, because
you've chosen it for its natural properties or
because it reminds you of a treasured time or
place. It could be driftwood you found while
wandering along the shore, a shell or pebble
given to you by your child or a crystal you've
chosen for yourself. Take your talisman with
you, in your pocket or bag. Whenever you need
soothing, hold it in your hand, contemplating
how it feels to the touch. Feel how your talisman
anchors you in your intention and deepens your
feeling of connection with your loved ones,
wherever you are.

16. MEDITATION ON THE BREATH

▸ When we breathe better, we feel better. This
simple breathing exercise promotes the healthy
functioning of your parasympathetic nervous
system – the "rest and digest" part of your nervous
system, as opposed to the "fight and flight"
response. Stimulating the parasympathetic
nervous system helps to mediate the effects of
stress hormones, so this practice is a simple way
to tap into a feeling of calm, anytime, anywhere.

If it is appropriate, close your eyes and set the
intention for the next minute to let the world
wait for you. If you can't safely take time out,
then carry on with what's required of you and
just work with your breath. Breathe in normally
through your nose, feel a little pause and take
a long, soft "ahh" through an open mouth on
your exhalation, elongating it only as much as it
feels comfortable. Keep this breathing practice
relaxed; over-exertion could agitate you. Spend a
minute experiencing your breath in this way and
consciously releasing any tension you might find.

17. KINDNESS STONES

▶ Seek out some smooth pebbles – you might
find some in your garden or head to your
local nursery or art supplies store. Grab some
permanent markers or waterproof paints and
get creative. Decorate your stones with patterns,
make them into characters or mark them with
qualities you hold dear – like "hope", "strength",
"peace" – or write an affirmation that speaks to
you. We have a whole family of stone ladybirds
adorning our garden.

Dip into your collection and carry one with
you as a talisman for the day or leave one
as a "kindness stone" for someone in your
community to discover. You might even find
a local Facebook group dedicated to this practice.
Join it to see the joy you've created.

18. GET CURIOUS!

▶ Curiosity frees up stuck, rigid thinking, giving us space to respond to situations with greater care and compassion. Developing the skill of curiosity is a powerful mood alchemist, helping us to see things from different perspectives and take things less personally.

To cultivate curiosity try this simple practice: when you face minor irritations in your day, use the phrase "I wonder..." For example, see if you can generate different, maybe more charitable, attributions for the behaviour of others. Ask yourself what might lie beneath the actions of others and consider a wide range of ways someone else might be feeling. Using the phrase "I wonder..." will help you question assumptions or quick conclusions that you've leaped to. Even just taking the time to think about a range of conclusions gives you a chance to cool off and choose more mindfully how you'll respond.

19. REACH OUT

▶ Feeling a sense of belonging is a cornerstone
of our well-being and we can feel bonded
effortlessly in an instant with this practice.
Pick up your phone and text "I'm thinking
of you" to the first person who comes to mind.
Or scroll through your photos to find a shared
memory. Send it to them and savour that joy
again with your friend.

20. A SIMPLE MOVING

MINDFULNESS PRACTICE

▶ Use this seated sequence whenever you'd like to connect with your calm abiding centre. Perfect to disentangle yourself from the busyness of your day before going to bed.

▶ Come into a cross-legged seated position on the floor. Close your eyes and take a few breaths here to drop your day. Place your hands on your knees and begin to circle your torso around your hips, making the movement as large as feels good to you. There is no right way of moving; allow your spine to arch, round or side bend as it feels comfortable. Take five circles in one direction, feeling the stretch in the sides of your lower back, before rotating in the other direction.

▶ Sit tall and move your arms with your breath. As you breathe in, raise your arms out to your sides and overhead, looking up to your hands to lift your mood. As you breathe out, bring your hands into a prayer position and lower them down in front of your body. Repeat this five times, feeling it calm and centre you.

- Now twist to release your upper back and neck. Breathe in and raise your arms skyward. As you breathe out, rotate toward the right, bringing your left hand onto your right knee and your right fingertips to the floor behind you. Hold here for five breaths, elongating your spine as you breathe in and twisting deeper with each exhalation. Keep your jaw parallel to the floor and gaze over your right shoulder. Breathe in, return to the centre and raise your arms skyward again. Breathe out and repeat the twist to the left.

- Sit for ten breaths in stillness with one hand on your heart and one hand resting on your abdomen. Feel your hands move with your breathing, the heat of your hands against your body and connect with the deep sense of calm that resides within you.

21. NATURE THERAPY

▸ Have you noticed how different landscapes have different energetic effects on you? Are there particular environments that speak to you with their soothing, grounding or invigorating properties? How do you want to feel? Turn to Nature Therapy and draw on the power of your environment to conjure how you want to feel. Visualize the environment that channels this, watch it in your mind's eye, pore over some photographs, watch a documentary or, better still, go there if you can. It's a matter of personal resonance but here are some ideas:

▸ Moving water to remove stagnation, cleanse and re-energize you.

▸ Still water to connect you with a sense of calm and clarity.

▸ The forest or woodland for a feeling of grounding, safety and stability.

▸ Open space to tap into a felt sense of freedom and possibility.

- Mountains or cliffs to channel strength, perspective, equanimity and resolve.
- Let the wind blow away your cobwebs.

- You could also try to:
- Observe the seasons to make peace with change and loss.
- Let crisp, cold wintery scenes invigorate you and awaken your senses.
- Savour the sensation of the sun on your skin and the transfusion of light and life through your whole body.

Self-care colours: use colours and their different energetic qualities to nourish you through your day. Draw on blues to calm you, greens to refresh, yellows to uplift, pinks to soothe and reds to galvanize you.

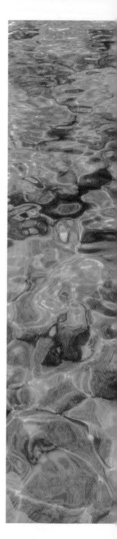

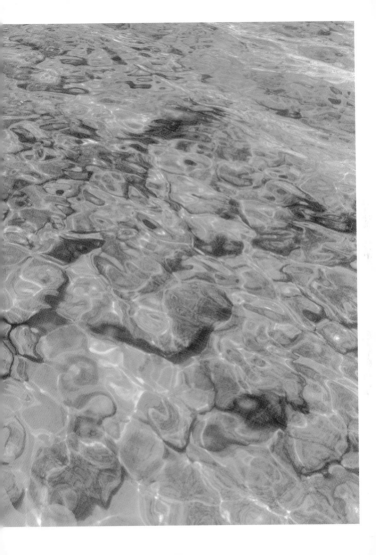

22. BRING MINDFULNESS

TO YOUR NUTRITION

▶ One of the easiest ways to bring self-care to daily life is to turn an existing behaviour into a ritual of nourishment. The way you eat your meals provides a perfect opportunity – you are doing it anyway, why not attune yourself fully to the sustenance it offers you?

Today, bring mindfulness to your eating and hydration. Everything that passes your lips, bring your full attention to it. This means downing tools, switching off screens and letting your "to do" list wait. Follow these steps:

▶ Slow down and tune in to the sensations of hunger and thirst that you feel. Notice the cues from your body and take loving action to feed your mood and fuel your body. ("Hanger", or the moodiness we feel when we're hungry, is real and impairs our ability to function.)

▶ Choose where you will savour your meal. Eating at your desk or in front of the television seldom creates a nourishing experience. Can you go outside or sit somewhere that you find naturally life-giving?

▸ Carefully select what you are going to ingest. Any doubts about what constitutes a healthy choice? Ask your "Future Self "– you in a few hours from now, tomorrow or a few months down the track, it's up to you. Which nutritional choice will bring you closer to who you aspire to be?

▸ Bring all of your senses to the act of eating and drinking – the colours, the aroma, the textures and flavours in your mouth, and the sensation of swallowing.

▸ Notice how much is required for you to feel satisfied and respect that cue.

▸ Reflect on how this practice went for you. Observe how it can help you make different choices and how it facilitates a different experience of eating and drinking.

23. YOGA TO ENERGIZE

▶ Try this short standing sequence to uplift and enliven you. A great alternative to that third cup of coffee and your adrenals will thank you for it!

MOUNTAIN SIDE BENDS

▶ Stand tall with your feet hip-width apart and your arms placed down by your sides. Notice how it feels to be standing upright, feeling the strength of your legs and the support from the earth beneath you. Imagine there is a pane of glass in front of you and one behind you, so you can't arch or round your spine, all you can do is elongate and side bend. Notice how good it feels to be standing so tall, giving a real sense of power and alertness.

As you breathe in, raise your right arm skyward with your palm facing you, stretching all the way up to your fingertips. As you breathe out, reach your right arm over to the left, making a banana shape with your body, until you feel a stretch through the right-

hand side. As you breathe in, bring your body back to upright. As you breathe out, float your right arm back down by your side.

Breathe in and raise your left arm up. Breathe out and reach your left arm up and over, banana-shaping your body and stretching the left-hand side. Inhale to return to centre and, as you exhale, float your left arm back down by your side. Repeat this action five times each side, moving slowly and deliberately with your breath. There is no benefit in moving fast. Once complete, notice if you feel taller than when you began and tune in to the energy that is now circulating around your body.

24. OUTER ORDER, INNER HARMONY

▸ The environment you live and work in has a
tangible impact on the quality of your mind.
Outer order really does facilitate inner harmony.
Scan your environment and notice what enlivens
you and what depletes you. What action can you
take today? Perhaps it is getting on top of life
admin by dealing with your in-tray or it could
be creating one place to keep correspondence,
invoices and important paperwork. It could be
as simple as a good dust and tidy of one area.
Brighten up a spot with some cut flowers or
invest in a well-placed houseplant. Commit to
cleanliness and order in your environment and
feel how this is reflected within. Notice how this
can transform your perception of cleaning too!
When I recognize how much better I feel after
a good tidy-up, cleaning feels less of a chore and
more like a refreshing act of self-care.

25. PURPOSEFUL ACTION

▶ Identify a value or a personal strength and set the intention to use it today. Think along the lines of a quality that's important to you or one that comes naturally to you, such as kindness, fairness, courage, compassion or zest. Throughout your day look for opportunities to bring this quality into action, feeling how the congruence with your values and strengths boosts your mood, your self-confidence and sense of peace. This practice helps you switch off automatic pilot and take more purposeful action. Even just the practice of articulating your strengths and values can be uplifting.

26. BE YOUR OWN CHEERLEADER

▸ Today, every time your inner critic pops up
or you face a challenge, tune into your inner
cheerleader – yes, you have one! Your inner critic
might feel more familiar, but I promise you, your
inner cheerleader is just waiting to be heard. If
you're having a tough moment, pause and ask
yourself: how would anyone feel if they were in
your shoes? How can you encourage yourself as
you would a buddy in this moment? What might
you say to someone else in this circumstance?

What personal strengths can you draw upon to
help you right now? Your inner cheerleader will
remind you and will help you clarify the right
action to take. There's no merit or benefit in
indulging your inner critic but don't bother trying
to silence that voice. In my experience, trying to
stamp it out just makes it louder. Remember, it's
just a thought, not your identity or some prophecy
of the future. Instead, let your inner cheerleader
get a look in. Practise the skill of offering yourself a
supportive and kind word and you'll see that great
things truly blossom from self-compassion.

27. MUSIC MEDITATION

▶ There is no denying the transformative power of music. Listen to something really old and dear to you and feel it transport you back to that chapter of your life. Tune into something that deviates from your usual playlist or something new to you and enjoy a different experience. Draw on various types of music to channel your desired mood. Listen to an upbeat song to energize, or consider classical music or meditative nature sounds if you need a moment of calm. Go all out and book a gig for a full-on sensory experience. Take someone close to you and you'll make some potent memories together.

28. PRE-BEDTIME WIND-DOWN YOGA

▸ Ditch screen time and swap it for this short floor-based yoga sequence to soothe and calm. A few minutes is all it takes to release your day and pave the way for a better night's sleep.

KNEELING SIDE PLANK

▸ Come onto your hands and knees. Step your right foot back behind you with your toes tucked under. Enjoy the calf stretch here for a few breaths. Set up your Side Plank by turning your right heel in toward you and grounding the whole sole of your right foot while remaining on your left knee. Slowly bring your right hand onto your hip and be prepared to wobble; this is all part of it. Stack your right shoulder on top of your left and stretch your right hand skyward. Balance here, smoothing out the edges to your breathing for five breaths before repeating on the other side. Notice how it's hard to think about anything else at the same time as doing this balance pose. The precarious nature really fine-tunes your mental focus, perfect for leaving your day behind you.

CAT AND DOG TAIL

▶ Stretch the front and back of your body with these dynamic movements. Starting on all fours, breathe in and come into Dog Tail, lifting your tailbone, looking forward and drawing your shoulders away from your ears. Come into Cat pose on the exhalation, rounding your spine with your chin to your chest and your tailbone pointing down toward the floor. Move smoothly between these two shapes five times.

THREAD THE NEEDLE

▸ Release your spine with these dynamic twists. Starting on all fours, take your knees wider than hip width and your hands to shoulder-width apart. Breathe in and raise your right arm up, stacking your right shoulder on top of your left and looking up to your right hand to create a twist in your torso. Breathe out and "thread the needle" by sliding your right hand, palm facing upward beneath your left arm and bringing your right ear toward the floor. Repeat five times, feeling the stretch in your chest as you reach up and the stretch in your upper back as you slide your hand through. Repeat on the other side.

WIDE-KNEE CHILD'S POSE

▸ Bring your body back to neutral with this soothing and calming forward bend. From all fours, bring your knees wide apart and your big toes to touch. Sink your bottom to your heels, your forehead to the floor and loosely drape your arms out in front of you. Surrender to gravity and enjoy the sensation of earthing your brow and breathing into the back of your body. Stay for as long as it feels good to be here.

Head to a charity shop and buy some little glasses or vases. Line them up and pop a couple of stems in each. This makes a lovely, inexpensive gift idea too.

29. MANTRA:

"I GIVE MYSELF PERMISSION TO..."

▸ Ever notice yourself saying "I shouldn't feel like this" or "I mustn't think this way"? Too often we give ourselves grief by denying our emotions or desires and, despite pushing them down, they leak out anyway. This mantra is about respecting that there is a time and place for all emotions and it's not the presence of emotion that's the problem, it's what we do with it that counts. It is also about helping you fine-tune your inner awareness so that you can take action to meet your needs before energetic bankruptcy hits or resentment boils over into toxic behaviour. This mantra will help you bring the skill of mindfulness and your values into daily action.

Here are some examples of how you might complete the phrase:

▸ I give myself permission to feel this loss. I'll sit with it like a friend for the next ten minutes and just let it be.

▸ I give myself permission to say "no" to the invitation from my friend.

- I give myself permission to say "yes" to that invitation!
- I give myself permission to switch off and observe a digital detox this weekend.
- I give myself permission to have an early night.
- I give myself permission to work, safe in the knowledge that I am providing for my children.
- I give myself permission to dream big and let the "how" come later.
- I give myself permission to take a break from worry and problem-solving for the next hour. Replenishing my energy bank will help me be more creative later.
- I give myself permission to stand firm and honour my boundaries.
- I give myself permission to speak my truth.
- I give myself permission to sit and savour this sunset.

30. LOOK UP AND TAKE IN THE STARS

▸ When was the last time you stopped to bask in the beauty of the night sky? Wait for a clear night, head out somewhere away from artificial light if you can and look up. No fancy equipment needed, just your naked eye or some cheap binoculars will do. If you want to focus on the moon, you'll see more detail when the phases of the moon are waxing or waning rather than when it is full. Download and print a star chart or use an app if you prefer. Seek out constellations familiar to you and feel how it connects you with your childhood memories of looking at the stars. If you're in a different hemisphere to the one you know, get curious about constellations new to you. See if you can tell the difference between planets and stars. Notice how contemplating the night sky fills you with awe, deepening your sense of what's important in life.

AFTERWORD

I hope you find these practices deeply nourishing and uplifting! Leave this book by your bed and regularly flip through these pages to see what leaps out at you. Take it with you so you have access to self-care on the go. Give a copy to a friend who is going through a tough time. Jot down your own nurturing practices in your Self-Care Journal and keep taking action to proactively tend to your health and well-being.

Just in case you need reminding – after all, guilt is a tenacious creature – self-care isn't selfish. It truly is the gift that keeps on giving. It's not me "first", it's me "as well". Let that percolate.

Much love,

Suz xx